The Meanderings of Bing

Lines From My Forehead

Tim Harnden-Taylor

Published by Saron Publishing in 2016

ISBN-13: 978-0-9956495-0-7

Saron Publishing
Pwllmeyrick House
Mamhilad
Mon
NP4 8RG

DEDICATION

This volume is dedicated to the loyal band of folk who have, by their kind comments, enabled Bing to chivvy the aged guv into trundling on with these 'events' and such!

Had it not been for Tom, Angela and 'an Arthur' who've gamely allowed such visits, these 'moments' might well have not occurred. To my dear friends and family, near and far, I value you all so much.

Finally there's Alison, who has somehow put up with upside-down snooker viewing and so forth, not to mention years of indecision from yours truly!
Let's hope there'll be more tales and a few good surprises yet to come.

CONTENTS

ACKNOWLEDGMENTS

Facebook has put me in touch with so many wonderful folk and also renewed old friendships. I do hope they know who they are. However, I must mention two. Alton Douglas, comedian, actor and writer has, from the early days of Bing, encouraged me to keep writing and also reminded me that Jazz has waited quite patiently for me to return and delight in my early love.

Frankly, without the enthusiasm of Penny Reeves, Bingo Little would still be viewed only on Facebook by his followers. Penny is not only a 'follower' but also a 'doer'. In short, whilst dealing with her own busy writing schedule, she has enabled the boy Bing to be released upon an unsuspecting public. Her patience in guiding this particular old dithering chump is positively saintlike, and if I ran the shop for dishing out such awards, she'd be at the front of the queue - Bravo Penny! I will never be able to thank you enough.

Tim Harnden-Taylor

Introduction

'Have you a moment, Bing?'

'Probabubberly, guv, what's afoot?'

'Twelve inches, ha-ha!'

'I've no idea what you're talking about, old wrinkly chops.'

'I see. Well, let's start again.'

'Right-ho.'

'The thing is, young lad, you need to supply an introduction for your book.'

'Hurrah and such! Just a couple of minor points, guv.'

'Yes?'

'What's an introduction? AND more importantly ...'

'Yes, Bing?'

'What's a book?' The gaze I get from the lad appears to be innocent and yet I can't help believing he knows very well their meanings.

'You know the shelves in my study?'

'The room where you go for a snooze and such, guv?'

I choose to ignore this slight.

'There are lots of shelves and on 'em are books.'

'Ah, so that's what they are. I've noticed you stare at them a lot when you're not snoozing.' Another slight to be ignored and ... I plough on.

'Well, most of them have an introduction.'

'I see ... so what's an introduction, guv?'

'It tells the prospective reader what to expect within the pages.'

'Well, blow me down.'

'And in your book, a bit about you.'

'Me? Well, I'm a hound that lives in Lowtown and my pals are Tom, Angela and an Arthur. I have various duties of course.'

'Duties?'

'Well, one very important one really.'

'Which is?'

'You know very well. Tom and Angela go to work while an Arthur goes to school and so forth. Meanwhile, I come to spend the day with you at least twice a week.'

'I see.'

'On the whole, old poop, you are quite well behaved but you obviously need the company of a hound to keep you on track. In short, to stop you wandering, staring into space and snoozing.'

'Oh I say.'

'You can 'oh' as much as you like, old puffer, but that is what I do.'

'And Alison?'

'Well, she's the sensible one in this 'ere establishment.'

'I see.'

'Do you, guv, do you?'

'I think so.'

'Right, so let's get this introduction sorted.'

'I think we've got enough for the moment, Bing.'

'Really?'

'Yes.'

'Tip-top, so how about a snack?'

'Snack?'

'Well, we book people require some form of sustenance.'

'Sustenance?'

'Certainly, guv, certainly.'

Bing has gone ... I'll find him sitting very neatly next to the snack tin.

Meanwhile ...

Welcome to the World of Bing!

Tim Harnden-Taylor

If You Happened To Be...

If you happened to be toddling along a particular path, enjoying the sights and sounds of this corner of England the other day, you may well have spotted a chap staring into space, accompanied by a hound trundling about in the close vicinity, inspecting the surrounds. I'm sure, around this dear old world, such events also happen and are not particularly remarkable. However, IF you had perchance stumbled upon this particular scene, you might well have been slightly disturbed, as these companions appeared to be in deep conversation and completely unaware of your presence. Sensibly you may well have decided to give this pair a wide berth and continue your jaunt. IF though, you were naturally inquisitive by nature and desirous of further knowledge of this event, you would naturally have found a suitable spot and observed the following ...

'Are you sure, guv?'

'Well, Bing, I know I had 'em when we started out.'

'M'mmm. Guv, as you well know, I'm not one to cast nasturtiums.'

'Aspersions, Bing.'

'Whatever. But it has to be said, your mind easily wanders and it's quite possible you might have nibbled on one and then, having got the *taste* for 'em, chomped on the rest!'

'Bingo, this is too much. I can be accused of many things but partaking of a pal's treats is most definitely not one of them.'

From your safe spot, you would have noticed the gent this time carefully check each pocket in the coat, removing various bits and pieces. This manoeuvre was repeated with the jacket beneath and then the trouser pockets as well. Meanwhile, the hound had trotted around the tree stump the aged gent sat upon and, snuffling around a particular patch, addressed his companion.

'Might this be what you're looking for, guv?'

'Good heavens, Bing, how did that drop out of my poacher's pocket?'

'Poacher's pocket? Cor, you live in another world! The only poaching you attempt, old poop, is with an egg!'

'Bingo, I am not entirely inefficient in pursuit of the old culinary delights and so forth.'

'And such like?'

'Quite.'

After this brief exchange, you would have spotted the dog's tail wagging as treats were received. After this, the gent went through a repeat performance of the pocket-patting routine, this time producing the familiar green tube known as *'Polo's the mint with the hole.'*

And there, I think we should leave them, both happily munching and contemplating the rest of their stroll. Whilst you wonder what all that was about!

Socks....

It's possible by now you will have realised my time spent with the Grand Basset Griffon Vendeen, known as Bingo, has probably been beneficial to us both. It has to be said, his questions about all that is new to him have made me reassess what I actually know about whatever it is he's questioning. This may, of course, be (as the Bible states) falling upon stony ground. If so - say no more. However, if, like me, you are amazed at just how much you take for granted until questioned on a subject, I'm delighted not to be on my own!

For instance, the other day I was ruminating on the fact that, not for the first time, I was wearing different coloured socks and whether anyone had or would notice, when the boy wandered into the study.

'What's up, Bing?' He looked at the ceiling.

'The light, guv.'

'No, I mean, what's going on?'

'The light if it gets dark.'

'Sorry, what I meant was, what's on your mind?'

'I've been thinking...'

'Ah right, thinking eh?'

'M'mmm.'

'Is it a matter I can help you with, old fruit?'

'M'mmm.'

I must say I was a tad taken aback. Bing usually gets straight to the point. For once, he seemed lost for words. In the ensuing silence, I shuffled some papers on my desk, sharpened a pencil and tried to look unconcerned.

'That's a funny business, guv.'

'What is?'
'Well, you stick quite a long bit of twig in that machine, turn the handle, and each time you pull it out you grumble, tut and put it back in again, turn the handle ... and it gets smaller and smaller. What's all that about and such?'

'It's called a pencil sharpener, Bing, it sharpens the lead in the twig, er ... pencil, so that I can write things and rub them out if it's not right.'

'Really?'

'Yep, it's pretty clever.'

'M'mmm.'

'You don't seem too impressed?'

'Hey, I'm a hound, twigs are for chewing, chasing and such business, not writing with.'

It was my turn to 'M'mmm'.

Moments passed ...

'The thing is, old poop,' Ah, now we were getting down to the real question. 'The thing is, while I was in the garden, I noticed a squirrel digging in a large flowerpot so when he bounced off, I popped over to see what it was he was up to.'

'I see.'

'You'll never guess what he was doing.'

'Well ...'

'He buried a sort of nutty thing.'

'Probably an acorn.'

'Really? I rolled it around my mouth and gave it a bite ... it didn't appeal.'

'Quite, it is an acquired taste, I believe.'

'Why would he do that?'

'Well, squirrels like to get ready for winter and so they spend some time each year, storing tit-bits to nosh during the cold months.'

'Well, that's mighty clever of 'em.'

'Yes, Bing, but their memories can be a bit faulty and so

they bury loads of things for the winter. The chances are they'll at least find some food, as and when required.'

'Ah ... so they're forgetful like you, eh?'

'What?'

'Well, old wheezer, judging by your socks, you forgot which colour you were going to wear today!'

'Ah.'

'Time for coffee and things, guv?'

'Things?'

'I'll show you where my biscuits are ... just in case your memory's a bit faulty!'

With one bound I leapt from my chair in hot pursuit ...

... he beat me to the kitchen ...

... but only by a long nose!

Waiting for Doggo ...
(with apologies to Mr Beckett)

Today it was a toddle up into the forest residing close by our house, Lyons.

'Why's it called that, guv?'

'Well, you see, it's a corner house ... ha ha!'

'That's funny?'

'Well, it could be called amusing. If you happen to remember the Corner Houses owned by Lyons.'

'Would Tom and Angela?'

'Er ... no.'

'Anyone else?'

'Well, you would have to be of a certain age to remember them.'

'Ancient like you, eh?'

'Hey, steady on, Bing, I'm not quite in my dotage yet.'

'You see, guv, using words like 'dotage' definitely ages you.'

'M'mmmm ...' It was time to change the subject. 'So do you fancy a stroll?' There was a blur before my eyes and within moments, the lad was sitting patiently beside the front door, drumming his tail on the doormat with impatience! Receptacles for bagging up any outdoor ablutions, (I hasten to say Bing's!), were slipped into a jacket pocket, lead located ... and we were off.

The sun was up and running so with a light heart we trundled up the slope and into the ancient forest. I panted my way up to the high beeches and sought a fallen trunk to regain some wind!

'You okay, old totterer?'

'Um ... (pant) yes ... I think (pant) I'll be fine in a moment.'

About forty feet away, two squirrels scurried about the newly fallen leaves and, quite clueless of our proximity, gambolled and bounded around. The boy watched all this with keen interest. Finally, having spotted us, they froze and eyed us from behind twitching noses.

'Cor, squirrels, eh, guv?'

'Cor indeed, Bingo.'

The grey duo bounded away and disappeared behind a large holly bush. We sauntered down the slope, in the distance a bridle jingled and soon the rider appeared, halted ... and the horse did what horses often do ...

'Blimey, guv, have you got a big enough bag for that lot?'

'Um ... I think we'll give that a very wide berth, thank you very much!'

'Oh.'

The rider tapped her helmet with her crop and being well bred, the horse, if it had possessed a hat, would, I'm sure, have raised it in our direction. Down the old familiar paths of leaf mould and finally back to the house. Okay, so I'm getting old ... but Lyons is not a bad name ... for those that get it! A little weary, I wandered into the lounge.

'No chance of a sit down for me, then, Bing?'

A Refreshing Moment

It looked like rain so Bing trotted in to say I ought to get my flags in. (My shirts were drying on the line!) This done, I wandered back to continue with my ... um ... well ... daydreaming. For those who've not seen the cluttered room I fondly call 'the study' and the old desk at which I can be found 'pondering', I hope that description will suffice. It was a little later, whilst leafing through some ancient scrawls, ditherings and 'mutters', that I became aware of a nudge on the knee.

'Ah Bing, can I help you?'

'Ancient puffer, you can as it happens.'

'What's the prob?'

'Would you think I've been pretty well behaved this morning, so far?' His earnest expression almost made me burst out laughing. I put on a thoughtful expression and the lad continued, 'I mean to say, I've busied myself in the garden, chased a pigeon or three, tracked a squirrel, watched a couple of red and brown'uns (robins) who were being very busy.'

'Right-ho.'

'I have watched some television, on which a couple of chaps poked at some coloured balls with sticks ...'

'Ah, snooker.'

'Whatever, and then decided it was high time you toddled out to the kitchen and made a coffee and topped up my water bowl.'

'I see.'

'And ...'

'And?'

'I might like a Bonio ...'

'Ah.'

'And I dare say you ...'

'Yes?'

'You might like one of those biscuits you hid in the middle cupboard on the top shelf behind a jar of dried macaroni and a packet of rice - when you thought I wasn't looking!'

'Good heavens, how did you ...?'

'I was pretty sure that was where you popped 'em and my hooter confirmed it earlier when you left the cupboard door slightly open.'

'M'mmm, I see.'

'Well, what do you think?'

'Amazing.'

'Really, it wasn't very difficult ... '

'No?'

'Hey, I'm a hound.'

In short, by the time I gained the kitchen, he was sitting nonchalantly next to the Bonio tin ... refreshments followed ...

... after which the lad decided to continue watching 'Ah, snooker'.

Snacks and Robbers!

The aged forest close to our home affords many delights for the stroller. Young as Bingo is, he's quickly become quite knowledgeable regarding local highways and byways and is always keen to learn more. When not out and about with his pals, Tom and Angela, he can sometimes be observed trailing an old 'wheezer' in his wake.

Recently I took him over to see 'Lowtown' Camp, an ancient spot still inhabited apparently by the locals at the time the Romans popped over, determined to stop us from painting ourselves blue and commencing construction of straight streets here, there and everywhere ... and so forth.

The lad was mighty interested in all this - until a squirrel whizzed past and whistled up a nearby beech. Having, as yet, not mastered the art of tree climbing, Bing gave a couple of low 'woofs' and we trundled back to the main path.

'So guv, those old blue geezers used to camp here?'

'Yep.'

'Why blue? Were they Chelsea supporters?'

'Um ... do you know, I'm not entirely sure.'

'Perhaps we could poodle 'em when we get back?'

'Poodle? Oh, Google 'em!'

'That's the chap. Perhaps he'll know the answer.'

'Possibly.'

We had, by now, reached the point where various paths cross and I was wondering if we should go in search of the 'Lost' pond or save that for another outing when my companion said, 'So who's this old bloater, Mick Gherkin?'

'Who?'

'You mentioned him the other day.' I racked my brain, trying to think who it was.

'You know, that robber chap.'

'Oh!' (The fog lifted) 'Dick Turpin!'

'That's the chap!'

'Well, he lived in this area and was a bad lad.'

'Coo, did he paint himself blue?'

'I don't think so, he came a lot later.'

'I see.'

'He was a highwayman.'

'I see.'

'He held stagecoaches up and robbed folk.'

'Crumbs, you mean he grabbed their food?'

'Even worse than that, Bing.'

'Not, not their Kit-Kats and such like?'

'Very likely.'

'Cor, what a bad'un!'

'Bad'un indeed.' Noticing the lad was looking a tad worried, I continued, 'Well, that's all in the past, fortunately. He won't be holding us up today.'

'Um ... have you got any snacks with you?'

'Well, Bingo, I did remember to pop a few "treats" for a certain pal, in my pocket.'

'Hurrah! Can I have 'em now, before old Gherkin comes by?'

For his sake . and that of history, I decided it was appropriate to *'Have a break ...'*

Tata for now.

Calm Sea and Preposterous Voyage

The piano is building as I reach the last verse ...

> *The bells they sound on Bredon*
> *And still the steeples hum*
> *Come all to church, good people*
> *Oh ... noisy bells be dumb!*
> *I ... hear ... you*
> *I ... will ... come ...*

(The last chord gently fades ...)

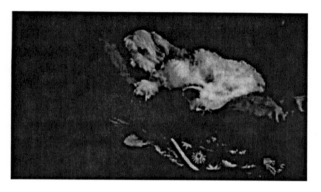

'Cor, there won't be a dry eye in the kennel after that, guv.'

'I think you mean "house", Bing.'

'Whatever.'

I've been trundling through a few tunes, a daily exercise in the hope that I can maintain a bit of lung function. In truth, other exercises, such as attempting 20 lengths of the local pool, would actually result in a gentle gravitational spiral to the bottom of the deep end. I must own, I never was a Buster Crabb or Johnny Weissmuller and definitely not an Esther Williams!! My swimming is a bit more secure when attempted as a stately backstroke in a favourite sun-drenched pool - and certainly far from any possible whalers!

In front of me, I spot some lyrics ... but of what? In vain, I pat the top of my head, hoping my specs are resting up there. The thought of the inevitable glasses search rests heavily upon me. A gloom descends ... and ... I decide to launch into the crash bang introduction of ... *Til Havs!*

Bingo rushes past, making a hasty retreat to the study.

'Oh, sorry, Bing, I forgot you were settled on the sofa.'

He calls over his shoulder, 'I'm off to batten down the hatches, Captain, and make sure the deck don't get pooped!' The notes crash out and off I go in ... uncertain Swedish! From the hall I hear ... 'Squeaky ball overboard, guv!' I can't be stopped, the surge of the waves and the wind is driving me on, on with the outgoing tide Ha - ha - HA! 'We're shipping water, guv, and the mainstay has sheared off the thinga-me-doodle and jibbed the flipperty-wotsit!'

Finally ... the storm passes and having given a final resounding *Til HAVS!* I drop anchor and decide a tot of rum (well, Pinot Noir) will slide down rather nicely.

I see Bingo peering in from the gloom of the hallway.

'Stack me, guv, that was better out than in!'

'Well, you know, Bing, every now and then one just has to ...?'

'Let it out?'

'Yes, Bing.'

'M'mmm.'

'You sound unconvinced.'

'Well, old poop, it's like this ... you know when every now and then, you wonder why I suddenly go bonkers and tear around chasing here, there and ups-a-daisy?'

'Yes?'

'Well, it's just me having a quick *Til Havs* moment, guv.'

'Fair enough, Bing, fair enough ... fancy a snack?'

'Always fancy a snack, guv, yes, definitely always up for that!

'Ship's biscuits it be, me lad!'

'Crumbs, guv, you're not going to get all nautical, are you?'

'Well, I might give you my Charles Laughton as Captain Bligh.'

'Who and who?'

'My Charles Laugh ... never mind, Bing, there's only a few who'd remember that particular *Mutiny on the Bounty*.'

'Bounty ... m'mmmm.'

'Bing, I'm not talking coconut bars.'

'Really, guv? ...

......well, I most certainly am!!'

Quackers and Honkers

The day was wearing on, the watery sun low in the sky, and the lad and I had recently returned from a stroll. I was sitting in the garden, sipping a cuppa and enjoying the end of the autumn day. A chin rested itself on my knee.

'What's up, Bing?'

His nose pointed upwards.

'Seems to be a lot of activity up there, guv.'

'Ah, well, you see, we're on one of the flight paths for Heathrow airport, and then other planes are making for Stansted, Luton and ...'

'No, guv, I was thinking of honkers, quackers and flappers in general!'

'Oh, geese and ducks, eh?'

'Very likely, guv.'

'Ah.'

'The thing is, aged poop, what are they all up to? I mean, why are they going this way and that, here and there and so forth and such like?'

'Well, most of 'em are off to other places for the winter. I'm not much of a 'twitcher', as we call folk who watch birds, but generally at this time of the year, our flighty friends decide to beetle off to places they most like to spend their winter months.'

'Oh.'

'We of course, on the other hand, rather like the old hearth and home. Ah yes, the delights of being snug and the prospect of Christmas with all the joys that can bring.'

'You're rambling, guv. I mean, I'm sure you're probably right but it makes a chap wonder whether he should be somewhere else?' I caught the earnest expression and tried my hardest not to smile.

'Bingo?'

'Yes, guv?'

'I think you know the answer really, don't you?'

'Well ...?'

'Would you miss not seeing Tom and Angela every day?'

'Oh, rather.'

'And let's face it, can you imagine what an old grouse I would be if you didn't spend time keeping me on my toes? And what would Alison think if you were somewhere else? Not to mention Pat at the stables!'

'Lummy, I hadn't thought of that, old poop.'

'Ah well, Bingo, just because some folk go flying off to other parts doesn't mean we all have to, eh?'

'You're right, guv.'

'Just think of how lazy I'd be if you didn't get me out and about.'

'Even when it's drizzling, guv?'

'Yes ... well ... um ... oh ... yes! Even when it's drizzling!'

The hooter sniffed the autumnal eve.

'I'm mighty glad I don't have to go who knows where.'

'I'm glad you don't have to as well, young Bing.'

'I'll remind you of that next time you're pretending to snooze and we should be out and about, guv!'

'I would never doubt it ... never doubt it.'

Autumn Leaves

We seem to have been having rather a pleasant walk this particular morning; the year wears on and autumn takes a real hold on the forest. We've been lucky; although it's cold, the sun is making every effort to brighten the day and the leaves that remain on the trees are responding, positively glowing in places.

The Boy Bing has once again patiently paused as the old wheezer behind attempts to keep up. Our efforts are now being rewarded by the frequently changing light and the response of the trees to this. We have settled into one of our regular strolls which have become very dear to me, despite the effort I have to make to keep up with the young'un.

'There's a good spot, guv.' The lad has noticed a rather good stump for me to rest on and as I sit, he is already gently reminding me that a halt in the walk indicates a treat or two. He does this by attempting to thrust his hooter into one of my coat pockets.

'Ah, Bing would be requiring a small treat?'

'Or two, guv ... or two.' I fumble in my left-hand pocket and he frowns, knowing full well that the treats this day are in my right pocket. 'Come on, old poop. Cough 'em up.' I repeat the process by delving into my right-hand pocket and he gives me a wink of approval. Nosh is transferred to the gently receiving mouth.

The crows are being particularly 'squarky' today and we've spotted several magpies which I gave up counting as I'm not sure how unlucky the rhyme is as we count at least eight or nine! Bing nudges my knee and gives a low cough, my cue to pass over the second treat. A single bell can now be heard tolling but by the time I'm aware of this, I'm not sure if it's telling me the time or announcing a funeral across the forest.

'You're a bit quiet today, guv.'

'Am I, Bing?'

'Cor, I should say so. You usually mutter away about the mud or tripping over branches and such.'

'Do I?'

'You know you do, ancient puffer.'

'I suppose I do.'

'Oh yes, it wouldn't be a proper walk with you if I didn't hear you huffing and puffing and generally muttering about something or other or such like and so forth.'

'Good heavens.'

A sudden gust and hundreds of leaves, confetti-like, shower down around us. Many different shades of autumn cascade down and gently come to rest on the forest floor, adding to the wonderful carpet we've been walking across. Bingo has a good shake and three or four leaves depart him for the carpet.

'I think, old gaffer, that before we trundle on our way ...'

'Yeeees?'

'That there's a certain chap not far from you who could be persuaded to nibble one last goody before we pootle home.'

'M'mmmm.'

'Come on, guv, you know it makes sense.'

'Sense?'

'Certainly, aged pappy, certainly.'

I can hear Alison saying ... *You're like putty in his hands.* And of course I am and of course the lad's tail wags for a third time.

As we walk home, I hear myself mutter as I trip over a half-hidden branch and notice the lad's smile ... all's well again.

In Good Queen Bess's Glorious Day!

We have, I believe, from time to time touched on the bridle paths and tracks that meander about the forest close by Lowtown. These ancient ways have been well-tramped over the centuries. Indeed, we have a hunting lodge once owned by Queen Elizabeth I which is now rather a nice spot for lunch!

I digress. Toddling along, looking out for wildlife and just enjoying the peaceful surrounds, it's hard to believe we're only 13 miles from Charing Cross. (Miles approximately gauged in my old Austin A40 back in the early '70's!). Folk of this sceptred isle have crisscrossed the area, ancient Brits, Saxons, Vikings, Romans and Normans have all spent time here and it is as if the trees have knowledge of all this and watch the current folk making their ways.

Here, this particular morning, Bing and the old codger sitting quietly are making our ways. I'm wondering if we might spot a deer. Skywards a jumbo jet, so high, silently leaves a vapour tail. Once again I'm wondering where it's bound and marvelling at all the people within.

'Hello, he's daydreaming again.'

'M'mmm?'

'I was observing, you were miles away.'

'Ah.'

'Cor guv, I sometimes reckon I couldn't half make you jump if I crept up and gave you a mighty woof!'

'Oh you wouldn't ... would you?'

'Might.'

'Oh no, you couldn't possibly ... could you?'

'Well ...' The lad 'paffed' my right hand pocket.

'I see ... bribery eh?'

'Hey, I'm a hound, a chap's got to do what a chap's got to do and I don't see anyone else around who'd be carrying a treat or two.' Did he wink at me? I'm sure he did. 'So, do I wait and make you jump or ... ?'

'Okay, let me see what I've got.'

'That's easy, aged guv, gravy bones right pocket, milky ones left.'

'How did you know?'

'Hey, I'm a ...'

'Hound. Right, got it.'

My companion very gently in turn relieved me of one of each. I peered into the undergrowth ... was that a movement, possibly a fallow deer? Good Queen Bess of course would have been seated upon a fine 'hoss' and able to see from on high any possible movements ... m'mm or there again ...

'WOOF!'

'Stone me, good gracious!' The old ticker was pounding and I was back in the day!

'Blimey, guv, you shot about three feet in the air!'

'Yes, well, I was ...'

'Daydreaming?'

'Possibly ... please don't do that again, promise?'

'Well ...'

'Oh come on, Bing, a fellow has to be able to ruminate.'

'Does he?'

'Most certainly.'

'Well ...?'

'Oh all right, let me see if I have any more in my ...'

'One of each in both.'

I gave up, gave in and gave 'em over.

'And Bing, no more WOOFS?'

'You're quite safe, guv...'

... for today!!

Brief Encounters ...

There have been times during our little outings when I've wondered quite what the boy Bing makes of our stop-start perambulations. For those of you who've journeyed with us, it must be painfully obvious that the old poop who trails behind the lad is probably not quite the sort of trundler he'd prefer. However, he has managed to slow down and make allowances for the aged guv. One plus of course is that he's learned to observe more than just the scents that percolate up the renowned hooter. We plod a number of regular trails and it's interesting to notice the changes as the seasons turn, as well as the wildlife and folk we come across during our jaunts.

Bingo is an affable sort of chap and is still not sure why squirrels don't wait around for a chat instead of scurrying up the nearest tree.

'What do you reckon all that's about and so forth, guv?' We are both peering up into a nearby beech at one of these 'furry flouncers'.

'I think, old fruit, they reckon we're after their winter nosh.'

'Coo, guv, I've tried their haycorns and such and am not impressed.'

'I guess they just can't believe we're not pining for such fare.'

The lad decides to use a bit of Bing diplomacy. 'Oi, you up there!' The squirrel leans forward, nose twitching. 'You're more than welcome to your nosh, we're not partial to it ... honest!' The squirrel lifts its head slightly and for a moment I'm reminded of the sort of face Kenneth Williams would have pulled! ('Oh ... Matron!')

By now, mine and Bing's necks are aching and the squirrel, I believe, is not going to play ball and pop down for a chat.

'Come on, guv, old sniffy up there's not interested.'

We continue on our stroll, both noticing the squirrel's

Shortly after, we meet two dogs out with their walker. They are a Jack Russell and a West Highland White Terrier, who are very bossy looking but actually settle down after a low woof! from the lad. Their walker is rather like me, so we are happy to stop for a moment and get our breath back.

He addresses us with a raspy voice, 'It's very muddy over by the stream.' This is confirmed as I notice his extremely muddy boots and trouser bottoms!

'Right-ho.'

'Mick, Monty and me are orf to the pub and a pint.'

'Sounds like a good plan.'

'Yus.'

We nod and orf, I mean off they go, and we wander away avoiding the stream. We later meet up with a young retriever and his young master and I tell them it's very muddy by the stream, and they thank me for telling them, and yet I can't help thinking they aren't at all bothered about a bit of mud ... and I feel even more of an old poop.

'What are you thinking of, guv?'

'Oh, nothing, Bing, just feeling a bit old.'

'Only a bit, guv?'

'Don't be cheeky!'

'Made you smile though, didn't I?' He had, of course.

'One cheering thought, Bingo.'

'What's that?'

'At least this forest is a lot older than me!'

Bing looks very carefully at me and then at the ancient oaks and beeches ... 'Are you sure, old puffer?'

Cox and Box and Suchlike

The boy Bing is generally a light-hearted sort of cove and full of bonhomie. There are, however, occasions when the lad will suddenly peer at something or someone with a definite frown and the sunny disposition momentarily disappears behind a cloud.

One such moment appears when Henry does. Henry is not the sort of critter that Bing is anxious to befriend. We try our best at Lyons to make sure, rather like Mr Bouncer and his tenants Box and Cox, that, as Mr Kipling (not the cake man) wrote, 'ne'er the twain shall meet!'

'He's a noisy sort of fellow-me-lad, guv, a right windy bloater if ever there was one ... and so forth.'

'I understand, old chap, but he is a necessity, I'm afraid.'

'G'rrrrrr.'

Sadly the comings and goings at number 67 are not the stuff of clockwork and there are moments when the inevitable will come to pass. Recently I was given instructions to chivvy up the cushions and shift the dust about a bit so events that coming evening could take place without a display of the usual chaos! In short, we were expecting guests!

My mate eyed me suspiciously as soon as I entered the lounge armed with a duster and proprietary can of instant shine from 'Mr Sheen'.

'Having a bit of a do, guv?'

'Apparently.'

'Will there be cake?'

'Oh, I would have thought so or something of that sort or

other.'

'M'mmm, cake.'

Having completed that part of the operations, it was time to tackle the floors, both wooden and carpeted. It is now that a frown appears and Bing sidles out of the room and takes the air in the garden. Words are not spoken but a look is sufficient to denote that the lad is 'not amused'. Vacuuming commences and a face appears at the garden door window, one great furrow over his brow ... and believe me, the lad can really furrow when required!

Finally I'm done and life can return to normal ... well, as normal as it ever can be around here. All is peaceful. I settle at the piano and trundle over the keys and peace descends.

PAFF! PAFF! the noise of a hooter hitting the window!

'Has he gone, guv?'

'Who?'

'Oh you know who ...'

'Okay, Guv?'

I had started to watch a robin hopping around being busy. Somewhere during my observation, my mind has wandered. (Hard to believe, I know!) I've been peering into the middle distance, pondering. Pondering just about covers the word, for I've been in this state for several minutes. Ash leaves are fluttering down onto the lawn and if the day were a bit drier, I might get the Flymo out and have one last trundle for the year.

'Okay, guv?'

The problem is that I need to look for the safety adapter for the electric mower and for the life of me I can't think where it's been left after the last cut. Frankly, it could be just about anywhere. The robin is now perched on the handle of the garden fork and he cocks his head one way and then the other. Fancifully I wonder if he is looking for the safety adapter - he certainly seems to be searching for something.

There's a definite chill in the air, November is all but over, and the tops of the trees in the ancient forest are displaying different autumnal shades. A helicopter clatters overhead as it returns to base and the very blue sky beyond is threaded with the trails of many jet planes.

'Oi!'

'M'mm?'

The clothesline has a very neat row of raindrops hanging from it, each one so clear and perfectly matched with its neighbour. It could be (I'm back with the safety adapter) back on the shelf in the cupboard where it should be or still plugged into the extension lead.

'Oooolffff!' Two front paws arrive in my midriff and I find myself looking at a familiar shaggy face, cocked to one side.

'Ah, you're back, guv.'

'I don't think I've been anywhere.'

'Cor, you were staring into space, old poop. I tried to get your attention but once you go missing, a paff's the only way to bring you back!'

The raindrops cascade from the line as the robin lands there and continues to cock its head this way and that.

'Hello, he's gone again.'

'M'mm, what?'

'I said, you've gone missing again, old codger.'

'Golly, my coffee's gone cold.'

'Surely you can't be surprised, guv, you've been standing there, miles away, for ever so long.'

'Oh.'

'What you need is ...'

'Another coffee?'

'Nope.'

'Tea?'

'No, no.'

'U'mmm.'

'A nice healthy stroll, that's what you need.'

'Really?'

'Nothing better, aged puffer.'

'Well?'

'Oh, you know you want to really.'

'Do I?'

The lad nods in the direction of the nearby forest.

'Let's get up there, guv, and you can daydream while I have a jolly good old sniff about and so forth.'

'Well?' I gaze into the cold coffee cup and then at the eager expression of the lad. I guess a stroll would at least take my mind off the last mow of the season and safety adapters ...

'It's just as well I have to keep you on a long lead, governor.'

'Really?'

'Certainly, old poop, certainly. Let's face it, once we get in the forest, you'd be hopelessly lost within two shakes of a squirrel's tail!'

'...And I...Shall Ne'er Be Lonely

As my voice and the piano faded away, a furry head popped up over the side of a 'napping' couch.

'Blimey, guv, that's a bit of a sad'un.'

'Bing, I didn't spot you nodding there. I thought you were in the garden.'

'M'mmm, well, I thought I'd have forty wags in here.'

'Right.'

'So those folk in Hughley are all under the ground, then?'

'Um, well, yes.'

'All a bit gloomy, ain't it?'

'Well, Bingo, the poet is recalling the friends of his youth.'

'Is this the same geezer who wrote of Bredon Hill, bells, daffodils and being twenty-one and such like and so forth?'

'That's the chappie.'

'Did he write anything about long lost treats, squeaky balls, chasing buzzers and whizzers?'

'Um ... I don't think so, not as such.'

'Oh.'

'He loved the county of Shropshire and often wrote about it.'

'Do you think you could drop him a line and see if he could write something about chasing squeaky balls? I don't mind if he pops a few daffs, roses and the odd bell in as well.'

'Um, well, Bing, that might be a bit difficult.'

'You mean, getting the lines to rhyme? I bet you could manage it, guv?'

'Well, I could have a go ...'

'Hurrah!'

'Um ... well ... let me see ...' The lad rested his chin on the arm of the couch.

> *Across the fields and forest,*
> *Where deer and squirrels dwell,*
> *You can hear the birds a-calling*
> *And squeaky balls as well.*

(the lad's tail wagged ... I pressed on)

> *The sound of Buzz and Whizz by*
> *The call of duck and drake*
> *Will echo 'round the woodland*
> *From stream to pool and lake.*
> *Here friends will ever wander*
> *And pals will never part*
> *While the sounds of ancient forest*
> *Reside within their heart ...*

'What do you think, Bing? Bing??'

The lad was fast asleep, dreaming of ... I tip-toed from the room and made a cup of coffee. I have a little tune to pop the lines to, so perhaps when the boy awakes, we'll give it a try ... meanwhile ... let sleeping dogs lie.

'C'mon Gaffer, Keep Up!'

The forest path is muddy, soggy and slippery. An ever-cheerful chap is looking back at the gloomy old poop trailing in his wake.

'Cor, look, guv, this tree has up-sticks!' (A large beech has come down, fortunately landing in an open area.) The panting, grumpy old huffer sniffs and wonders if there's any chance of a breather. The boy Bing, undeterred and as bright as ever, positively dances along the trail oblivious to the doom and gloom *humphing* behind him!

Of course, it's only natural. Here we have a hound, bred to be impervious to all that the elements can chuck at him, followed by an old poop, not so bred and longing for the delights of a cosy room and a steaming cuppa! By the pond, the ducks are huddled among the reeds and sensibly staying out of the biting wind. We notice some bubbles and the lazy roll of a fish. A thrush is nearby and a pair of blackbirds are about, their feathers ruffled by the wind.

'Isn't it luvverly out here, guv?'

Lovely? M'mmm ... lu-vver-ly ... that's not quite the description I have in mind. A tree decides to rid itself of surplus droplets just as I'm passing.

'Oh, nuts!' My companion is far too delighted with a new smell to hear me. Lu-u-u-vver-ly? It's late November, the sun has most definitely not *'got its hat on'*, the clouds are loading up for a mighty downpour, yet again I've forgotten a scarf and my ears are 'barking'!

Bing trundles on and we cross a bridge that might have harboured a troll underneath ... if it wasn't so blasted cold! We have settled into a rhythm and are making fair progress, given the conditions. Lu-u-uvver-ly? (The old grump's still musing.) We have the forest to ourselves this morning, nobody's silly enough to be out and about.

I nearly trip over the lad. He is stock still and looking dead ahead. There in a clearing stands an old dog fox, with white cheeks and chin and much of his red coat now very grey. He has a front foot raised and is listening to the sound around him. We dare not move and we're hardly breathing.

He hasn't spotted us and with his head slightly raised, he's slowly sniffing the air and we can see the steam from his breath. A bark in the distance and the old chap cocks an ear, deciding on which direction it came from. Slowly the front foot returns to the ground and he moves forward a few paces. His ears prick and suddenly he has become aware of the hound and the old puffer.

This is an old fox, he's seen it all and frankly a couple of strollers are really of very little interest to him. He trots towards us and then turns slowly to his right, cocks a leg and leaves a mark, before wandering off into the forest depths.

'Well, guv, he was a big'un.'

'He was indeed, young Bing.'

Once again the forest has reminded me not to be such an old duffer and enjoy whatever it has to offer, no matter what the season. I look down at my companion who is still looking in the direction of the old fox trail.

'I reckon, guv, he's off to the old Lowtown Camp you showed me in the summer.'

'Ah, you remember that, Bing?'

'Oh yes, blokes painted blue and such like and so forth, not to mention old Mick Gherkin!'

'You mean Dick Turpin.'

'Probably, old poop.'

'I think you're right, Bingo. It's a good place to live, plenty of cosy spots and nice and peaceful.'

'See what I mean, guv, it's blooming luvverly out here, lots to see and for chaps like me, plenty of hooters full of tasty smells!'

He's right, of course. We've been lucky enough to see a little of the wildlife that resides on our doorstep, all for nothing ... well, except for a bit of effort from the grumpy old poop!

And So To Bed ...

'Spill the beans, aged poop! What's all this about old Pappy Christmas and all that and so forth and suchlike?'

'Well, Bing, it's like this, every year on Christmas Eve, those that have been *very* good during the year ...' A brow becomes furrowed. I continue '... will more than likely receive a special present from Father Christmas.'

'When you say **very** *good*, ageing guv, what do you mean?' I'm trying very hard not to grin as I look at the earnest expression and slight trembling of the lower lip.

'Well, young scamp, I should think that, providing a young chap receives a pretty decent report from a certain aged poop, then the jolly old gent in red will cough up a suitable present or two.'

'Or *TWO*, guv?'

'Maybe even three *if* the bearded wonder is particularly taken by the report received.'

'Crumbs!'

'Crumbs indeed.'

'M'mmm. So in your considered opinion, ancient fruit, would you think that, by and large and so forth and such like, taking all in all and allowing for the odd slip or three, that the lad before you might be considered as *reasonably* in line for such a beneficial coughing up of goodies?' It's my turn to 'M'mmm?' 'After all, historic relic, surely he couldn't fail to take into account my patience as I tow a wheezing geezer out on his constitutional?'

'Um?'

'I mean to say, chaps like me keep oldies like you on your toes and such.'

'Well?'

'*AND* let's face it, Tom and Angela would vouch for my exceptional behaviour at other times.'

'Exceptional?'

'Cor, not half, guv. I don't like to squeak my own tennis ball but at the end of the day, frankly if I don't, who will?'

'Well, Bing ...'

'Yes, guv?'

'I reckon you should be ... *just about* ... okay.'

A tail wags furiously.

'Hurrah! *Just about* is good in my book, old puffer, I'll take *just about* over *not very likely* any day of the week!'

(Somehow, I reckon the lad will wake on the 25th and not be *too* disappointed!)

And ... the 'tail' continues ...

... and so forth and suchlike.

The Descent of Man
... and Ladies!

Somewhere, back in the annals (of Bingo), I seem to recall mentioning that, if he were Sherlock Holmes, the lad, when pondering, instead of being a *two-pipe solution* chap, would be a *couple or three largish Bonios* sort of fellow.

I mention this because the other morning, after the usual excited greetings and trundle about the garden inspecting any new scents, the boy returned to the comfort of a couch. Here he became engrossed in a succession of young ladies hurtling down a twisting, turning icy run on what appeared to be little more than a small tray!

The lad turned to me and said, 'Good grief, old codger, can you believe what they're up to?'

I had to admit I couldn't and we lapsed into silence as another competitor whizzed off at high speed, careering around banked bends and clattering on several occasions into the icy walls of the run!

On completion, the eager new 'convert' turned to me, 'It's so fast, guv, I can't see what they're chasing!'

'Chasing, Bing?'

'Quite, old poop.'

'I don't believe they're chasing anything, dear lad, just seeing who can hurtle down the track fastest.'

'Really, guv?' The surprise in his voice was quite something and I could tell he was perplexed.

'Why, oh ancient and wheezing huff and puff, would they choose to beetle down such a track without having something to chase?'

'I guess, Bing, because *it's there.*'

He went silent and I could tell we were indeed in the middle of a *couple or three largish Bonio* contemplative moments! Finally, he looked at me and wrinkled his hooter a little.

'Guv, I will never understand you chaps.'

'Really?'

'Really, old bean. It has, guv, been remarked upon in this and other households that chaps like me engage in the practice of bounding, pouncing *and* bouncing here, there and ups-a-daisy, for no apparent reason ... and yet, guv ... and YET, here we appear to have seemingly sensible young ladies, choosing to slide with extreme gusto down a deadly slippery slope on a tea tray AND *not* in pursuit of anything other than *time*!'

I of course answered sensibly, 'U'mmmm.'

'U'mmmm indeed!'

I naturally attempted an explanation. (Will I never learn?)

'Well ... you see, Bing ... er, when some folk find themselves in snowy surroundings and when hurtling down hills with a couple of planks tied to their feet begins to pall ... they look for other ways in which to negotiate the pull of gravity! This can be by the construction of very slippery slopes, banking snow and designing conveyances to achieve a suitably exciting thrill.'

It was the lad's turn to 'U'mmm'. Fortunately, his eyes hadn't started to glaze over, which is frequently the case when I try to explain puzzling matters to him. He rested his chin on a paw and continued, 'In short, oh wizened one, you're saying it's quite okay for folk to practise such apparently ridiculous perambulations but chaps like me will be commented upon if we should take it into our heads to gambol and leap when rejoicing with the scents and delights of the moment?'

(Come on, H-T, for goodness sake, don't say um ... er!)

'Um ... er ...'

(Blast it, I did!)

The lad, *Perry Mason*-like, rested his case and suggested it was snack time.

Just between you, me and anyone else ... I think I'll try to avoid the TV channels currently showing any outrageous snowboarding events ... not for Bing's sake ... but my own!

Once More Unto the Beeches ...

'So what's all this interest in the weather, old huff and puff?'

We are both gloomily looking out of the window at the steady rain beyond. I'm thinking, *There's no way you'll catch me out there in that stuff.* The eager lad next to me is naturally thinking just the opposite. I know that the following passage of time will be a-fraught with the struggle of *'Two mighty monarchies, Whose high upreared and abutting fronts, The perilous narrow ocean parts asunder'.* In short, once again, the lad will attempt to trick (this is not too harsh a word, given past occasions) to get the aged guv to acquiesce to his carefully constructed shenanigans!

The steady pitter-patter of raindrops on the window pane are to me like nails being driven into the lid that will be put upon the lad's efforts. The boy Bing sighs, he huffs, grumps a little and gets down from his observation point and with a sad backward glance at the old poop, he wanders limp-tailed from the room, leaving me the momentary winner.

Can I be turned from my present course?

Absolutely not!

Can my hard demeanour be altered by the pleading of a possible opposite view?

Certainly not!

From the hallway just outside the study, I hear a long sigh.

Is there any thawing in the cold defiance I'm determined to retain?

Nope.

A single rather sad squeak rends the air as, through the crack in the door, I see the lad resting his chin on his favourite rubber ball. His brow is slightly furrowed and another sigh joins with a second squeak

I notice from the sparkling pane that the rain has eased off and a pale sun is attempting to cheer the scene outside. The *'front of house'* sparrows have regrouped and are now chattering around the lawn and shrubs. A large damp cat wanders by, not on the hunt, just wondering if anyone has noticed its bedraggled state. We have!

And now? Well, a rainbow is straddling the distant view and everything is looking rather green and pleasant. Two pigeons, regulars around Lyons in Lowtown, are sitting on a fence in deep conversation and probably enjoying the unexpected warmth.

I'm aware that it is mighty quiet out in the hall. Peering through the crack in the door, I see the lad appears to have disappeared. I decide to wander out of the study and possibly pop the kettle on or ...

In the hall by the front door stands the boy Bing, tail wagging fit to whack seven bells out of the walking stick stand!

'Now, Bing ...'

'Oh yes, please, guv, now would be really good.'

'My use of the word *now*, young fellow, was not meant in the sense of *this moment*, rather it was to emphasise a point I was about to make.'

'Which was, old white bonce?' (Where he gets these expressions from, I have no idea.)

'Well ...' (Blast, I've lost my thread.)

'The lead is parked on that chair, guv.' He nods his head in the direction of one of the chairs close by.

'Yes, well ... er ... we can't be ...'

'Out too long?'

'Quite ... um, yes, absolutely ... quite.'

Our exit from the house is observed by the sparrows briefly

and by the two pigeons, one of whom, like all other pigeons, finishes his song in mid-coo! The lad? Well, it's no surprise really, he's full of eager sniffs and wags as we trundle the familiar pavement. And the loser? Only on this particular occasion, I do assure you, is making every effort to keep up with the 'herbert' in front!

February

Over in Lowtown, the weather is extremely wintry. The old gent who attempts to keep the young lad entertained is actually longing for an upturn in temperature, whereas the boy Bing is impervious to the cold and continually perplexed as to the inability of the old puffer to keep up!

Fortunately Bingo spent yesterday at stables near Epping. He and the 'gang' trundle around the yard, being most observant of the 'stable mates'! The horses are mighty patient with the antics of the 'pack'. In fact, all the dogs are extremely well-behaved around the horses and ponies. They seem to realise that here, the stable takes priority and, provided they 'behave', all is well.

I tell you this because after a day at the stables, the lad is quite happy to spend the next day 'pootling' around the house, whilst keeping half an eye on any sporting events emanating from the box in the corner of the lounge.

'Guv?'

'Yes, Bing?'

'Being of an aged disposition, old poop, I was wondering if, somewhere tucked away in your memory, you might recall where we might have stored the blue and white 'squeaking' ball?'

'Well, young man, given the sharpness of your hooter when it comes to sniffing things out, I'm surprised you require the jaded conk of yours truly.' He looks at me as if I've finally lost it!

'Crumbs, old boot, I just thought it might do your brain a bit of good to work out the location of the marvellous "pill"!'

I settle on the settee and as I get comfy, a loud 'squeak' rends the air!

'There you are, oh great crumbling one. I knew you'd get there in the end.' M'mmm, why do I get the feeling that a certain chap sitting close by has deliberately popped the ball under one of the cushions?

Moments later, I spot Bingo outside trundling around the lawn with the ball, getting in some practice for when his pal Tom arrives home from work and some serious 'ball play' can take place. In the garden, various flowers are popping out the ground which in itself brings solace to the old poop ... the year (if rather too slowly for me) is edging on and slowly nature is responding and I must be more patient.

A hound whizzes by the lounge windows and a 'favourite' ball is getting a really good workout. The boy Bing, oblivious to the changing year, is just delighted to be here, there and ups-a-daisy. He's as full of beans as it's possible to be!

Come on, Spring, I know you're about somewhere ... it would be rather nice if you popped over sometime soon!

Hey-ho.

Never a Crossword!

Having finally managed to cut the green stuff which in this weather laughingly calls itself a lawn, I decided it was time for a brew and possibly a little treat. It was while I was reposing on my favourite couch, carefully nibbling around the edges of a two-fingered Kit-Kat ... well, we all have our little pleasures ... that my furry pal sidled through the lounge garden door clutching his current 'favourite' stick!

'Bing, I fear Granny A will have something to say to you if she wanders in.'

'Really, old puffer - I just plan to gently gum it, there will be no mess ... we can't all have Kit-Kats, don't y'know.' Suitably contrite, I placed the offending confection next to my steaming cuppa and returned to my crossword. M'mmmmm ...

'Stuck?'

'Well, no, not really ... just pondering the possibility of a trick answer.'

'I see.'

Time passed ...

'Oh all right, cocky, I might be a tad unsure of an answer.'

'Stuck.'

'Well, yes, if you must know, I just can't make head or tail of this clue ... 12 across: **Reverse taxi out of cutbacks and you'll get marooned!**' Bing lent his chin on his stick and gazed at me ... a look of patience and great benevolence on the noble visage.

'Another name for *taxi* is *cab*, *bac* backwards out of *cutbacks*, and what are you left with?'

'C U T K S,' I blurted out!

'Now, what word does that make that means *marooned*?'

'Um ... er ... oh ... *Stuck*!'

'Exactly!'

Well, folks, I was flabbergasted ... the boy Bing rested his chin on my knee.

'As that chap in the advert says, "Simples!" '

'Bingo, I can't thank you enough ... though where you got this knowledge for crosswords from is frankly extraordinary!' The lad picked up his 'favourite' and wandered back out into the garden, as Alison entered ...

'Has Bingo been eating his sticks in here again?'

'M'mmmm?'

'It looks like a family of beavers have been at work!'

'Well, no, he just, um ...' I gazed down at the bits of chewed wood.

'Honestly, you spoil him terribly ... have you eaten that Kit-Kat already?'

I turned to the cooling cuppa with familiar red wrapper and neatly rolled ball of silver paper ...

'Um ... yes, I guess I did.'

Alison frowned ... 'Have you seen today's newspaper?'

'I left it on the kitchen table. I didn't want to see the answers to yesterday's crossword.'

'Well, it's not there.'

'M'mmmmmm ...'

Later, as I was wandering over the 'lawn', I spotted something white in a flowerbed. I was staggered to find it was the daily paper ... open on the answers page!

I have my suspicions but let's face it, who'd believe me?

Arts and Crufts

'I've been thinking, guv.'

I'm not sure how I should react to such a sentence from the boy Bing. I certainly have to try and remember that, being a hound, the lad has a tendency to view matters from a slightly different angle to homo sapiens.

'Thinking, Bingo?'

'Certainly, governor, certainly.'

The clear eager eyes are observing me and for some reason, I find myself back in the classroom where, as a lad, my mind was apt to wander. Suddenly I'd come back to earth and find myself looking into the enquiring eyes of a teacher who'd just asked a question to which I hadn't a clue as to its nature, let alone have a suitable answer! I brace myself and thus our conversation progresses in this manner.

'And um ... what have you been thinking about?'

'Well, it's like this, old poop, ever since Crufts the other day and that magnificent win, I've been wondering why it is that yours truly hasn't been available for such an event and so forth and suchlike?'

'And have you come to any conclusions, Bing?'

'Frankly, I'm mystified, guv.' By now, my mind is racing and I'm wondering if I can find a suitable reply to the lad's stunning question.

'Well, it's like this, Bing ...'

'Yes, guv?'

(Inspiration, please fall upon this aged poop's brow. A small thought flutters down from who knows where.)

'You know when we return from a stroll and because of the wind, rain and muddy puddles etc, it becomes necessary to give you a thorough drying and ...' (Thank goodness my mind's working) '.... we then have to tackle the business of giving you a jolly good brushing from hooter to tail?'

The lad's eyes narrow suspiciously. I press on. 'Well, let's face it, young fruit, you're not exactly the easiest chap to brush, are you?' He blinks and the pressing continues ... 'Bing, can you honestly say that you'd be prepared to be brushed and brushed and brushed again, in order to appear in such a state that would be suitable and to the liking of the folk who do the judging?'

'Well ...?'

'You have what I would term a natural charm but I fear in truth you are not the chap for titivation and smelling like roses.'

'Blimey, roses, guv?'

'Well, all the entries into the competition are the sort that love being brushed and generally dandified to appeal to what the judges own to be correct.'

'Stone me, old poop, my gob has never been so smacked!'

'Bing, you are a natural with the um ... er ... sort of breeding ideal for what you do!'

'Well, I'll be blooming well blowed.'

'Be well and truly bloomingly blowed, young Bing. Leave Crufts to those that feel comfortable with it, you are ... number one in a field of one!'

'Blimey.'

'Blimey indeed.'

The lad's eyes, which had widened as the old poop had built up to a suitably grand finale, looked pleased with my pithy summation. Feeling that I was on a roll and on tip-top form, I decided to see if there was anything else I could help the lad with.

'Well, aged wheezer, as it happens, there is something else.'

'Ask away, young Bing, ask away!'

'Any chance of a snack or three?'

Mr Kear

'The piano man cometh!'

I was sitting listening to one of Bach's cello suites, when Bing sidled into the study. Having enquired as to who and what it was, he gave a slight nod of approval and strolled out to the hallway and sat very patiently - in expectation of what?

Well, it appears he at least was paying attention when Alison said, 'Remember, we are receiving a visit from Mr Kear this morning.'

In short, as we are halfway through the year, we were due a visit from Mr K, who comes twice a year to tune the piano.

When he arrived, I introduced Bing to Mr Kear and the pair disappeared into the lounge to inspect the 'instrument'. The lad was mightily impressed by Mr K's ability to shift the pitch of a note by means of what he felt certain was the starting handle for an old Bentley! I retired to make coffee while Bing stood on the settee, front legs resting on the top of the backrest, entirely thrilled with the aforementioned 'bent' notes – tail wagging and head cocking first one way and then the other.

Time passed and gradually Mr K worked his way from bottom notes to top of the piano, tweaking them as required. Finally, various scales and trills announced the piano was fully restored to the best of health. As Mr Kear sipped his coffee, he said, 'Bingo has been telling me all about Bach.'

'Really?' I said nervously.

'Oh yes, old "JS", as he calls him, is one of his favourites.'

'Really?' I said even more nervously.

'He's particularly partial to his "Jello Sweets"!'

Mr K's shoulders shook, the boy Bing rolled onto his back and fair hissed with mirth!

'Ah,' I said ... ' Welcome to the world of Bing!'

The Flowers That Bloom in the Spring

'Rum, tum ... tiddly pom, rum tum ... tum tum tum ...'

I was rum, tum-tumming along the other day, fully in a world of my own, when the lad's chin rested on my knee.

'Stone me, old poop, what are you rum-tummin' and so forth about?'

Naturally I was *slightly* embarrassed by this question, as I'd thought Bing was busying himself in the garden.

'Ah, yes, well ... Bing, yes, well, er ... ummmm ...'

'Is this an occasion when I should assume you were in the process of thinking up one of your tara-diddles, guv, or were you just pleased about something?

I was stuck. Frankly there was no new tara-diddle on its way and frankly I was unaware that I was rum-tumming ... until the lad broke into my reverie. I stared hard out of the window in the hope that a sensible answer would hove into view.

Nothing.

'Well, guv, while I have your undivided attention, I wonder if you could answer a thought I've had?'

It was no good, not a single vision had hobbled into view, not a tit-bit nor scrap of a thought could be conjured up ... in short (not for the first time) I was clueless! I gave up the attempt and turned to the eager face in front of me.

'Yes, well, Bingo, naturally I'm always ready to help with any particular poser you may have.'

'Hurrah, guv, you're back with us. Right, well, it's like this, old fruit. When I was out in the garden just now, I was aware that things seemed a tad different.'

'How do you mean, Bing?'

'Well, guv, everywhere seems to be, how can I put it? it's er ... sort of waking up, so to speak and so forth.'

We strolled out into the garden and inspected the surrounds.

'Indeed it is, young lad, yes, indeed it is. We are, and I choose the words very carefully, we are *finally* seeing the welcome entrance on the scene of spring!'

'Spring?'

'Yes, young scamp, it is that time of the year when plants and trees and dare I say it, grass ... are stirring themselves and so is just about everyone else!'

'Golly.'

'Do you remember back in the autumn when you spotted those high flying birds making for warmer climes?'

Er ... probably not, old poop, but if you say so ...'

'Oh, I most definitely do. I seem to recall you were a tad worried about where those folk were off to but very pleased when you realised *we* weren't going anywhere.'

'M'mmm ... I *think* I sort of remember, guv.'

'Well, some of the *high flyers* are already back and soon the old forest will start to leaf up and look delightfully green once again.'

'I love the forest, guv.'

'Bing, I would never have guessed!'

'Oh yes, it's great and just the place for a hound to get some serious sniffing in!'

'Quite. Now, what was it I was doing ...?'

'Not a lot, guv, just pom-pomming and such.'

Yes ... and the answer was of course, that *I* was full of the joys of spring!

...........AND about time too!!

Up In The Sky, Ever So High ...

High, high in the clouds, the sound of a long haul flight could be heard as it played peek-a-boo with the glowering skies. Above our heads, the newly arrived beech leaves were rustling on swaying branches, as they've done each new spring for centuries. On larger branches, every now and then, animated grey fur bounded along, tails aiding balance as each creature went about its business. Below all this, a 'guv' stands and smiles wistfully, as only an old poop can at such a scene. Meanwhile, even lower down, a hound trundles about, delighting in the fresh scents afforded by this new day.

Those who have wasted a little time with us on these rambles will by now have realised that not much really happens and somewhere around this old world, folk are doing similar strolls and, perchance later, they will see the same long haul flight passing over their heads.

The aged gent is particularly chirpy this day for a nearly full tube of Polos has been discovered in his old coat pocket and shortly the boy Bing will be even more chipper when he discovers the old poop has remembered a small snack or three.

Below, a few rooftops of old Lowtown can be glimpsed through the trees in one direction, whilst a turn of 180 degrees shows the ancient forest stretching away into the distance. It's playtime at the local school and across the wind comes the general hubbub of children.

This reverie is broken by a nudge on the knee.

'Hello hello, he's back with us.'

'What? Oh, Bing, what's afoot?'

'About 12 of your inches, guv.'

'I asked for that.'

'And it was duly delivered, old poop.'

The lad has recently had a 'short back and sides' and is looking leaner and fitter than ever. Frankly, since then, he's been looking most pointedly at my hair and I get the impression that a 'subtle' hint will be made in the near future. I decide to try and take his mind off me!

'I must say, Bing, you are looking quite different after your recent trip to the salon.'

'Well, guv, the staff are mighty friendly and take a good deal of trouble.'

'Good, good ... rather like Rossini's barber they were civil? Ha ha, do you get it, Bing? Barber? C-I-V-I-L? Rossini? Oh my, that's a gem, ha ha!'

I receive a look of great puzzlement but still a soppy grin remains on my face.

'Guv, even for you, that was pretty terrible.'

'Really? ... Ha ha, it's tickled me no end ... Ha ha!'

The noble brow looks kindly upon me and I'm suddenly aware that any passing stroller would be puzzled by an idiot cackling to himself whilst a dog looks on with great compassion! An attempt to compose myself is made and I stall for time by proffering a snack to the lad.

Folks, I put my light-headed state down to the delight of spring in the air. For, despite strenuous efforts, I found it extremely hard to regain a suitably sensible demeanour and the glimpse of a smirk danced upon my lips as the lad finished savouring his savoury.

'Are you all right, guv?'

'Why yes, of course I am, I'm quite, quite myself once again ...'

'M'mm, well, I don't want you frightening the ducks and such.'

'Bingo, I do assure you I am quite in control, quite, quite ... yes, yes ... quite.'

The lad's eyes narrowed as he sniffed in my direction most pointedly before turning and trundling down a path that would ultimately bring us to the duck pond. I towed along behind and with each step, made every effort to regain a sensible face and forget the poor pun. Engrossed as I was, I failed to spot the unexpected muddy pile of leaves and slipped and slithered some distance before managing to stop forward momentum by sitting on my bottom. The lead went slack and ahead I saw the broad grin of the newly trimmed hound wagging his tail with great mirth!

'Now, old poop, THAT is funny!'

I regained my vertical position with as much dignity as I could muster and laughed uncontrollably ... despite the nearing duck pond. My companion led the way along the well-trodden trail, tail wagging. He, delighted with my pratt fall ... and me, remembering Rossini's barber!!

Shush! ... say nothing!

Pond Life

The boards of the wooden bridge rumble slightly as the aged gent, led by the hound, trundle across its span and see the pond hove into view. The lad in front sniffs the air and his tail slowly wags.

'The ducks are at home, guv.'

In truth I'd never doubted it as it's quite some way to the next pond and I reckon these ducks aren't that adventurous. I could, of course, be quite wrong. However, they are 'at home' and we move quietly around one side of the pond to a landing stage. (It should be noted the ancient meander that flows into and out of this small expanse of water is not navigable so the landing stage is something of a mystery.)

I don't recall ever seeing the two families that share this spot, the Coots and their upper crust neighbours, the Khaki-Campbells (the hyphen is entirely my own!), sunning themselves upon the boards but as the lad and I aren't here every day, this statement may well be inaccurate.

As we emerge from the forest, there they are, 'taking the waters' and quite uninterested in our appearance. The Coots nod their heads, rather like 'Egyptian dancers' (I'm recalling Wilson, Keppel and Betty!) and the K-Hs glide sedately around the pond sides, carefully 'dibbing' at the shallows next to the reeds.

Bing enjoys this spot and is quite happy to take on board the sights and scents that float up the receiving hooter. I, on the other hand, am delighted to take a break and enjoy noting any changes in the plant life, trees and shrubs in the immediate surrounds. The lad is at the full extent of his long lead and sitting close to the edge by the water. The Coots are quite close, and is that murmured conversation I can hear? I'm far too polite to listen in so I gaze at the newly green-topped trees and take a few grainy photos on my ancient Nokia! For once, it is delightfully warm just here. Time gently floats by, as does my mind which has wandered who knows where? If one could gain an M.A. for mind wandering, or perhaps a B.A. for daydreams, this old poop would be the shop for 'em!

My reverie was rudely interrupted.

'Oi, muddybum!'

I believe regulars will recall the recent incident when I had defied forward momentum by landing on my bottom in a damp spot.

'What?'

'Stone me, I thought I'd lost you for good. There must be loads of fairies around here 'cause you were well away with 'em, guv!'

'Well ... um ... no ... I was ... er ...'

'I've been prodding and hello-ing you for ages, old poop. I even gave you a deep woof but you just kept staring at the tops of those trees over there.'

'Did I? Surely not.'

'The Coots have been cackling with laughter at you and as for the K-Hs, they sympathised with the job I have, keeping you from wandering off.'

'Oh I say ...'
'Well, you're back with us again which is, I guess, a sort of blessing.'

'Charming.'

'Don't mention it, old fruit. Now, if you're quite back down to earth and not liable to drift off back to the tops of those trees, is there a possibility that a chap might have a snack or four?'

'Snack or three, I think you'll find.'

'M'mmmm ... Well, it was worth a try, guv.'

(It was my turn to m'mmm.)

Going to the V-E-T-S

I was chatting to Bingo's regular pals, Angela and Tom, the other day and discovered that a certain hound (within hearing distance) was due to go to the ... um ... V-E-T's later that day!

The word V-E-T is even worse than those other dreaded words 'N-O Bingo!' In short, the lad is always aware of where he's heading in his transport module/pod. Frankly, we cannot be too surprised by his amazing ability in ascertaining exact latitudes and longitudes at any given moment ... for a hound he most definitely is!

Cutting a short story even shorter, it's on the occasion of a visit to *you know where* when *you know who* is at his sharpest. Naturally T and A try any number of cunning distractions in the hope that knowledge of the exact point of arrival is delayed as long as possible. This is of course to no avail, for the hooter of the Grand Basset Griffon Vandeen* is second to none!

Whether the upper or lower road is chosen, it isn't long before a look forms on the noble brow of *you know who*, and a glance from anyone who dares take a peek is returned with one of displeasure.

Arrival at the *you know what's* coincides with Master B leaping out of the car and making a general tour of the car park with the air of one who means to go anywhere but towards the entrance! Fortunately, once the door to the venue is open, the unmistakable (to a hound) whiff of minty-type treats percolates up the receiving nostrils and acts as an enticement to any chap on the lookout for a tasty tit-bit.

Once inside, he is greeted by the very pleasant ladies with many *hello's* and *how-di-do's*, and within moments the furrowed countenance becomes sunny once again and all is right with the world. Quite why dogs are so averse to visits to the V-E-T's is something of a mystery. I choose to believe that, once a chap has entered one of the 'rooms', a veil should be drawn across such intimate moments. Inspections to one's nether regions, such as earflaps, hooters and more sensitive areas, are not of interest to us, dear readers, but perhaps explain the reason for recurring appointments being the answer to a chap's reluctance to venture to the V-E-Ts!!

Since his 1st* birthday and the receipt of a blue pointed party hat, Bing has decided he looks like a Wizard; in fact, not unlike Dumbledore! Somehow, the breed as far as Bing is concerned, is now actually 'Grand Basset Griffin**dore** Vandeen!'*

TOWIE and Such Like

The commuter belt destination of Lowtown lies within a major *TOWIE* (*The Only Way is Essex* for those fortunate enough to have missed this particular 'delight') filming location. Fortunately young Bing is completely unaware of such goings on. It is, however, 'not unusual' to see some extraordinary apparitions teetering about the local Highroad.

Naturally, I would be defined as *'well old!'* Sadly, such utterances would be made by those ignorant of the gorgeous girls of the '60s and '70s that cheered this aged guv! Back then, it was not the fashion to spray oneself orange or to believe the height of sophistication is to carry some poor little 'mutt' around in (as Edith Evans would observe) *'A Handbaaaaaag?'* I shan't go on for I'm painfully aware of being hopelessly out of tune with these times.

That little diatribe came about because recently the boy Bing and I decided to drive over to Southern Lowtown for a leisurely 'trundle' around the playing fields. And so 'it came to pass' that we observed the efforts of an 'orange' young lady in extraordinarily high heels, grappling with the tremendous camber of the Highroad! Having attained with enormous effort the halfway point, the downward slope was tackled with all the deportment of a large stork wearing roller skates! The cameras were rolling but I fear this fascinating performance will be left languishing on the cutting-room floor.

'Stone me, guv, is that some sort of game?'

'I don't think so ... not yet.'

'I've never seen anyone attempt to move in so many directions all at the same time.'

'M'mmmm.'

Shortly after, we parked the car and Bingo led the way as usual while I made every effort to keep up!

'I see the "kick and chase" nets are up, guv.'

'Yep.'

'What's that roped area for, aged poop?'

'That's the *table* of the cricket pitch.'

'Ah, Crackit!'

'Quite.'

'Is that where they serve up lunch and teatime?'

'Um ... no, it's called the table as it's the area where the groundsman prepares the wickets.'

'And they are?'

'The designated strips upon which the bowler ... um ... er ... bowls.'

'All seems a bit complicated, don't it, guv?'

'Possibly but that's what it's all about.'

I believe the boy was about to tie me up in 'sporting knots' when suddenly his ears pricked as a shape streaked towards us, hotly pursued by a harassed walker! Excited greetings were given and received and eventually the pair calmed down and, having passed the time of day with the harassed walker, we trundled off in different directions.

'Mighty fine young lady.'

'A cross-poodle cocker spaniel, Bing.'

'Not cross, guv, just a bit excitable.'

'M'mmm, it was (giggle) ... that was a bit of a "Cocker-Poodle-Do" - eh? Ha ha!'

The vast expanse of playing fields engulfed my laugh, and the emptiness gathered it in as if the event had never occurred.

'You're an odd sort of codger, ain't yer, gov, and that's a fact!'

This might very well be so but I can't see things changing ... and that, most definitely ... *is* a fact!

In An English Country Garden

There is nothing quite like a summer's day on this island. I say this because it's not a regular experience, given the vagaries of our weather. It's simply gorgeous, making the pleasure of being part of such a day something to be savoured. Tea, coffee or whatever your tipple is tastes quite different when savoured outside. Perhaps the pages of a book or newspaper will gently flap occasionally in sympathy with a gently passing breeze. Certainly such a delightful scene can gently fade as the god Morpheus makes one nid-nod, with the sounds of summer gently supplying a murmuring soundtrack.

A familiar hooter prods the knee of an old poop who's away amidst *'golden slumbers'*. If not with the fairies!

'Is that you, guv?'

I awake with a start!

'Oh yes, it is you, guv. I thought we had a giant buzzer in the garden.'

Slowly the aged gent comes back from his forty winks and looks down at the enquiring gaze of the boy Bing.

'What? Me buzzing?'

'Certainly, gaffer, certainly.'

'I hardly think my gentle slumbers could be likened to a giant buzzer!'

'Well, guv, I heard a passer-by liken the sound to a buzz-saw.'

'Well, now you are just exaggerating, Bing.'

'Please yourself, guv, I merely pass on the comments of

others. I have to admit, though, that the noise coming from your hooter was not unlike the sounds we sometimes hear out in the forest.'

'Oh, well, now you're just being silly, not even I can sound like a chainsaw, Bingo.'

'Please yourself, they say the truth can sometimes hurt.'

'M'mmm.'

'Do you fancy another cuppa, guv?'

I look down at the empty mug and then at the lad.

'No, I don't think I do.'

'Really? Just think of that pot going to waste, guv.'

'Might this concern have something to do with a certain chap's snack?'

'Or three, guv, or three.'

'Well?'

A chin is rested on my knee and I receive an appealing gaze.

'Oh, all right then.'

'You know it makes sense, guv.'

By the time I trundle into the kitchen, the lad is sitting next to the snack tin, just in case I might have forgotten where it was!

Forest Murmers

Wandering the various paths of the forest called Epping, I've rapidly realised that, despite his young age, young Bing has, by dint of his noble breeding, rapidly committed to memory the tracks that criss-cross this famous plot. For even when we are travelling fresh ground, he appears by sixth sense to have a fair inkling of where we are and what may occur next! I cite as an example an event that occurred the other day as we trundled along in our usual manner, him up ahead sweeping from left to right and back while I puffed along behind as fleetly as I could.

Frankly, Bing's opinion of my tardy perambulations in his wake would fill more than this brief page. Therefore, let us draw a veil over that observation and pass on to other events - merely observing that young B's muted grumbling and occasionally eye-rolling in my direction are sufficient barbs for an old codger like me!

We were just reaching the crest of an incline when the lad dropped into a crouching position as if he were about to leap onto an unsuspecting squeaky pill. I stood still and within moments, two horses and their riders appeared from a path over to our right. A bird flew up from the bracken but neither horses nor Bingo moved. I was just about to mutter something like 'what a fine pair of chestnuts' when the boy rose and wandered over to them. I was at somewhat of a distance so couldn't quite make out the conversation taking place. After some seconds, the horses nodded and toddled off across our chosen path and the lad padded back to me.

'Very interesting, aged guv, those ponies were asking directions for the Lost Pond so you can imagine I was mighty pleased to be able to put 'em right.'

'Ah, so those were ponies, not horses, then?'

'Coo, you ain't 'arf a townie, ain't yer, old wheezer?'

Remembering my couple of rather shoddy efforts at horse riding many decades ago, I was apt to agree with him. AND what if I am a townie ... I'm very proud of dear old London and we can't all be cowboys or jockeys.

'You're daydreaming again?' the lad observed.

'Well, yes, I suppose I am, it's a problem I've had since I was a boy myself.'

'Paws!'

'What's that?'

'Paws or in your case hands ... that's how you tell the difference, old puffin!'

I started to grin and prepared to deliver my little quip ...

'Surely they have hooves, not paws ... eh ... ha ha!'

The lad cocked his head and peered at me - frankly for one so young, there are times when our roles become reversed and it is I who am left with the feeling he teaches me far more than I can ever teach him!

But then a dandelion clock exploded in a sudden breeze and the young chap leapt in various directions attempting to catch the floating seeds ... and life delightfully returned to normal.

Well, almost.

Slouches on Couches

We had returned from the morning forest trundle and having had a light lunch, I was settling down to continue reading a book. My walking companion was lying on the other couch, viewing the television in the corner of the room, on his back!

'You should try this, guv.'

'Really?'

'Certainly, guv, it brings a whole new view to sport and so forth.'

For some reason known only to other idiots, I rolled on my back and attempted to view the screen.

'Good heavens, Bing, I see what you mean. I'm not sure I would want to watch all the time from this angle.'

'Really, old fruit?' The incredulous tone in his voice made me wonder if it was at times like this that one realises the difference between man and dog.

'Well, Bing, the thing is, I'd find it hard to drink a cup of tea at this angle.'

'M'mmmm.'

'I mean, dear chap, I think most folk would draw the line at attempting such a feat ... it's nigh on impossible.'

'Long straws would do it, guv.'

I considered this for more than a moment or two and realised it might just be possible. It then occurred to me that straw or no straw, why would I want to?

'Cor, guv, you've changed colour.'

I was starting to feel a tad giddy and carefully regained my normal sitting position. The doorbell rang. I reeled toward the front door, blood finding its way back to where I guess it should be! The meter man stood before me, meter-reading gismo clutched in his hand.

'Ah, hello ... um, right, the meter's down here.'

I started moving various items away from the area, including a bag full of tap shoes! Slowly but surely, the under stairs door started to appear. The meter man waited patiently, he's obviously used to this performance at many houses. I started to feel rather like Howard Carter as he finally broke through to the Tomb of Tutankhamun!

The door finally allows itself to be opened. He flashes his torch at the gas and electricity meters and the job's done ... he goes. Then the task of placing everything back begins. I mutter something about clearing this area away so that next time it will be easier to get to the meters, knowing that I will, of course, go through the same routine next time!

'Crickey, guv, that was a bit of a performance.'

'M'mmm. I must clear this stuff away ...'

'That's what you said last time.'

'I know, Bing ... I know.'

'Hey, there's some 20/20 Crackit coming on in a moment ... that'll be great upside-down!'

Tea mug recharged, I return to the lounge ... Bing is in position ... I consider trying the upside-down viewing position, then realise Alison will be home shortly and it would not do to find us both at such an angle ... after all, I certainly don't want to appear silly!

Frogs, Buzzers and Whizzers

One afternoon quite recently, I spied young Bingo rolling in a sunny patch of grass and could see he was greatly relishing this particular exercise. 'Ah so, young fella, enjoying a bit of late warmth?'

The squirming lad froze and peered up at me through his shaggy brow.

'Frankly, old guv, apart from various squeakers, settee snuggling, noshing, chewing wood, noshing little treats, rolling in hay, minty chews' (The list was growing by the second) 'chasing ol' puffers like you, sniffing flowers, stalking buzzers and whizzers, drinking out of puddles, walks, snoozing ... rolling in the sunshine is pretty near the top of a young chap's list!'

informed, I strolled over to a seat in the sun while Bingo continued his rolling.

A few minutes later, I was nudged by a nose ...

'You old'uns like a snooze or three, don't you?'

'Well ... I was just resting my eyes.'

'Golly, does that make you rumble through your snout like that?'

'Um ... well ... was I?'

'Cor, your hooter was sounding like a pack of bees with colds!'

'Ah yes, well, um ... there you are.'

'Yes, I most certainly am, old wheezer!'

Taking the hint, I spent the next few minutes tossing his most favourite squeaking ball as far as our limited garden would allow. Suddenly he froze and stared into a clump of Golden Rod. 'What's up, young feller-me-lad?'

'There's something new blinking at me.'

I strolled over to the spot and stooped. There crouched next to the ball was a frog!

'It's a frog, Bing.'

'By a frog, you imply that there may well be more of 'em?'

'Oh yes, they are quite common in gardens and are regarded as being the gardener's friend.'

'Really?'

'Are ... are they ... friendly, guv?'

'Oh yes, no harm at all. They do have a habit of leaping up into air when least expected ... otherwise they are generally harmless.'

As I spoke, the frog jumped about a foot into the air which made my companion shoot backwards and assume a position behind me with just his nose poking through my legs.

'G ... golly, I see what you mea ... they come a bit sudden and make your ticker go blur for a moment, don't they?'

'Quite right, old fruit, but as I say, quite harmless and jolly useful in keeping garden pests at bay.'

'M'mmmm ... what, and more importantly ... how big are these pests?'

'Oh, just the size of whizzers and buzzers and smaller.'

His worried countenance cleared ...

'Oh, they sort those out, do they ... well, that's mighty pal-like, ain't it?'

'That's why they are the gardener's friend.'

'I see ... so they don't tug up weeds and shave the grass?'

'No,' I said sadly, ' ... that's left to others ...'

It was later, while 'shaving' the grass, I saw young Bing leap backwards and realised he'd just re-encountered the frog!*

*I later discovered Bing has decided to call him 'Cardigan'! Because, as the lad explained 'it' is a sort of a jumper!

Stratford and Such Like ...

'So what's all this and that about Stratford, guv?' Having spent ten minutes attempting to chase Master B around the garden, I was just taking my ease and enjoying some much-needed sunshine when this poser was thrown at me.

'Now, by Stratford, Bingo, do you mean the home of old Will Shakespeare the Bard, or Stratford, home of the 2012 Olympics?'

'Blimey, guv'nor, is there more than one Stratford?'

'Lummy yes, young B, they're all over the blinking world ... mainly to commemorate Bill the Bard.'

'Was he a good runner or something then?'

'Well, history has not enlightened us as to his particular sporting prowess. I guess he might have been pretty fit in his youth. He mentions (non-squeaking) tennis balls somewhere in Henry V but he spent most of his life in the theatre writing and acting within a wooden 'O', as they were wont to call it!'

'I have absolutely no idea what you're talking about ... cor, you don't 'alf trouble a young lad's brain with your words!'

'Ah yes, well, it's all part of a young chap's education ... let's forget about that for the moment and concentrate on Stratford in East London ... and the Olympics, eh?'

'Right, so what's all the fuss about?'

'Well, every four years, an event takes place when all the best runners, jumpers, throwers, swimmers ... not to mention rowers and ... oh, I don't know, you name it, and whoever is good at it, will be there ...'

'Squeaky ball chasers?'

'Um ... er ... well, I'm not sure ...'

'Do you mean to say there's no squeaky ball chasing or retrieving of any kind?'

'Um ... er ... well, I'm not sure ... I don't think so ... er ...'

'M'mm, it seems to me we dogs are being discriminated against!' I had to think fast as the lad had got quite a point.

'I think that you dogs have rather cornered the market when it comes to chasing and retrieving.'

'Ah I see, yes, well, I can see the logic in that ... it is something that we are past masters at. In fact, we pass our masters most of the time, eh? Ha-ha WOOF!'

'As ever, Bingo, you have hit the nail on the head.'

He immediately looked at the recently-applied elastoplast on my thumb.

'Whereas you seem to be good at hitting your thumb rather than the nail ... eh? ... ha! ha!' I looked at the plaster ruefully. 'Sorry, old huff 'n' puffer, I shouldn't make a joke ... but, cor lummy, you didn't half hop about the other day when you did it!'

The picture of that moment came to mind. Frankly, I thought a brief moment of hopping whilst hugging the afflicted left thumb under my right arm pit, better that the usual oaths and expletives that Shakespeare would most certainly have understood ... but not a young, impressionable hound like Bingo!

(So - that was the Olympics, it seems.)

One Poor Paw

'Bing?'

'Yes, guv?'

'I'm a bit mystified that you haven't made any comment about your altercation with that buzzer.' The lad looked at me, sat and thought very hard.

'No, I can't think what it is you are alluding to.'

'Ah, I see ... um, is the memory too hurtful?'

'Um ...' Again the boy looked very hard at nothing in particular, wrinkled his hooter and 'umm'ed' several times. I was about to change the subject when there was a sort of 'eureka' moment!

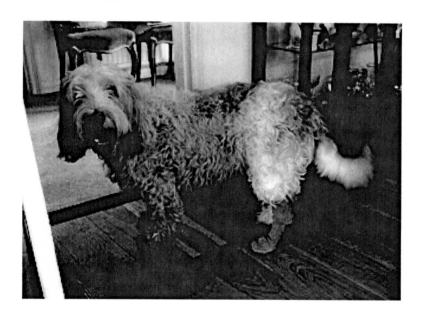

'Oh, you mean the stinger, guv!'

'That's the chap, Bing.'

'Well, to be honest, old poop, it was a tremendous shock at the time. There I was trundling about, minding my own business, and feeling rather pleased as the day was very sunny and the grass smelt luvvery, and having sniffed a few of those bright coloured thingummy whatsits ...'

'Flowers?'

'Those are the fellows ... and such like. Anyway, I was trundling towards a suitable spot, bathed in sunshine, for a short 40 wags when ... I felt something in my foot that made me almost leap over the garden fence!'

'Really?'

'Well, I can't be absolutely sure but it was mighty high and when I landed, my paw was fairly throbbing like a good'un.'

'Lummy.'

'Lummy indeed. Frankly, I found it quite hard to put my paw down so I limped into the house and told Angela and Tom!'

'Crumbs.'

'No crumbs, guv, not even a small treat. Naturally they had a look and then decided to take me up to the *you-know-where*, and have it looked at by *you-know-who*.'

'I see.'

'As you know, guv, the *you-know-what's* is not my most favourite place ...'

'I can't think why, Bing. After all, the ladies there always make rather a fuss of you.'

'Well, yes, that's true ...'

'And let's face it, even the *you-know-him* is rather a cheery sort of cove who quickly sorts out whatever it is that needs looking at.'

'That's true ... here, who's telling this tale?'

'Sorry, Bing, do please carry on.'

'Well ... um ... oh, you see, I've lost my thread now, where was I?'

'At the VE ... the place up the hill?'

'Probably ... um ... yes, that's it. I was naturally soon telling them about this most curious event and they were, I have to say, very sympathetic and I of course limped beautifully!'

'Oh, Bing, you didn't!'

'Certainly, guv, certainly.'

'Was it that painful?'

'What?'

'Your paw.'

'Oh yes, although I did at one point realise I was limping on the wrong paw but I don't think anyone noticed.'

'Bing, really, I'm quite shocked!'

'Hey, I'm a hound, guv, a chap's got to make his point as best as he can.'

'M'mmm.'

'Well, you did ask, guv, and it really wasn't very nice but Mr *you-know-who* found the stingy bit and pulled it out.'

'I see.'

'Naturally I put on my most noble look and departed the scene to a round of applause.'

'Really?'

'Abso-blooming-lutely, guv ... well, that's how I remember

it AND I know the ladies were very sad to see me leave.'

'Well, Bingo, I hope in future this experience will teach you to keep a sharp eye out when you are trundling about.'

'M'mmm.'

'M'mmm??'

'Well, guv, I think it was you, I feel sure, who managed to stub his toe on the leg of the piano the other day!'

'Well ... um.'

'And, let's face it, that piano is blooming huge compared to the buzzer I trod on!'

'Well ...'

'*And*, dare I point out, it is always where it is ... it doesn't move around ... not even slightly.'

'Ah, yes, well, you see ...'

'That's it, guv. I see it, the whole blooming family and any visitor sees it, and yet the old poop manages to clatter into it!'

'M'mmm.'

'I rest my case.'

And there I think we will leave that particularly painful event. The lad has forgotten all about the sting ... but my toe is still throbbing.

I've Been Thinking, Guv ...

'I've been giving this a great deal of thought, guv ...'

'Really?'

'Well, it occurred to me a moment ago but I reckon I've thought it before, because it seems sort of familiar.'

'I see.'

'The thing is, old poop, do you have an invisible pal?'

'Invisible pal? I'm afraid you've lost me there, Bing.'

'Really? You see, I've noticed you regularly seem to mutter away and I can only think you must be talking to a party or parties unknown.' Yet again, the lad astounds me with these sudden phrases ... clearly he's watching too many *Midsomer-cum-Morse-cum-Taggart-cum* ... well, you get the idea.

'Are you sure?'

'Indubitably, old cough drop.' I really ought to limit his telly watching when at Lyons for the day.

"Well, *IF*, as you say, I do happen to mutter, I'm merely making a comment to myself.'

'A sort of verbal *aide-memoire*, guv?' Perhaps I ought to suggest to Tom and Angela that he really is even more impressionable than we all thought?

'Bingo?'

'Yes, guv?' I am faced with the clear, unblinking gaze of the lad, to whom we humans must be something of a mystery.

'Well, the thing is ...'

'Yes, guv?'

'It just becomes a sort of habit.'

'Habit?'

'Yes ... you know, when you do something without thinking, instinctively.'

'I see ... I think.'

'Well, Bing, as you get older, I'm sure you'll become just as big a mutterer as me.'

'Lummy.'

'Lummy indeed, Bing.'

'Frankly, guv, I find that very hard to believe!'

I leave the lad looking a tad puzzled. I seem to have relocated to the hall and find myself suddenly unsure of why I'm here.

'M'mmm ... Now, what was it I was about to do?'

'See, you're doing it again, guv!'

I jump out of my reverie and see the lad grinning up at me.

'Ah, yes, well ... um ... er ...'

'I rest my case, m'lud!'

'Okay, Rumpole, you've made your point.'

'Rum-who?'

'You know jolly well *who*, young lad.'

'I'm sure I've never set eyes on the old cove and that's the truth, the whole truth and nothing but ... er ...'

'The truth?'

'Well ... okay, guv, it's a fair cop.'

'Time for a snack?'

'Or three, guv?'

'M'mmm.'

ABOUT THE AUTHOR

Born in London NW8 and now living towards the end of the red underground line in 'Lowtown', he trained in Birmingham as an actor and singer, later enjoying several years in the professional theatre, both in the provinces and in London's West End. A lifetime's love of classical music eventually found him at the old store in Oxford Street at HMV. Computers were still in their infancy, therefore an encyclopaedic knowledge of recordings was a must. Other jobs have followed and the need to write/scribble has always been there. Oh to be organized!

Enter Bing, and his enquiring mind. The journey continues......